Stuff Every

GROOM

Should Know

Copyright © 2015 by Quirk Productions, Inc.

Library of Congress Cataloging in Publication Number: 2014947244

ISBN: 978-1-59474-797-7

Printed in China

Typeset in Goudy and Monotype Old Style

Production management by John J. McGurk

10 9 8 7 6 5 4 3

Quirk Books
215 Church Street
Philadelphia, PA 19106
quirkbooks.com

Stuff Every

GROOM

Should Know

By Eric San Juan

QUIRK BOOKS
PHILADELPHIA

To my wife, Natalie,
who had an easier time stifling her laughter
the second time around

Introduction:
So You're Getting Married

Somehow, it's happened. You found someone who can tolerate your idiosyncrasies. Someone who laughs with you, not at you . . . usually. Someone who, inexplicably, has found it in her heart to love you.

Yeah, she's probably just as surprised about it as you are.

But for now she's still caught up in whatever delusion has taken hold of her, so you're going to do the smart thing. You're going to marry her before she comes to her senses.

You're making the right choice. She's a keeper. She puts up with you, after all.

You're also making the right choice reading this book. Any woman worth marrying is worth marrying well. She's already given you so much, and you're about to spend the rest of your lives together. So we're here for one reason and one reason only: to help ensure that everything from proposal to honeymoon goes as smoothly as possible.

And make no mistake, the advice in this book does not apply only to male/female marriages. For the sake of convenience we've stuck with those pronouns, but we suspect you'll find plenty of helpful advice here no matter the mix of your marriage.

Being engaged is a (usually) short but intense period full of important decisions and relationship-building moments. People are going to treat you differently. They'll have all manner of wisdom, both good and bad, to share—including this book. As for you, well, this is the first step in changing your entire life, isn't it? So best to get it right.

But don't worry, Groom-to-Be. Read. Observe. Learn. And when people ask, "Do you really think you're ready for all this?" repeat after me: "I do."

Engagement
Stuff

Choosing the Ring

You've found the perfect mate, now it's time to find the perfect ring. That little band is more than a sinkhole for a chunk of your salary—it's a symbol of your love. Here are some tips for making your quest a success.

- **Set a budget.** Before you start, figure out what you're willing and able to spend. As of 2013, the average engagement ring cost about $6,000. If you can afford that much, great. But it's easy to find a suitable ring for much less on the retail market or even in the resale or handmade marketplace (see "Other Points to Consider," page 16). Tell the jeweler your ideal range to help narrow your choices and avoid the "it's perfect but it costs too much" blues.

- **There is no right amount.** The diamond and wedding industry will say that you must spend two months' salary on a ring— nonsense. Pick the right ring for your future wife, not one based on an arbitrary number. And yes, prices are negotiable. Don't be afraid to haggle.

- **Know the Four Cs.** Carat, color, clarity, and cut are the four factors that determine a jewel's quality. Clarity is how clear a stone is, color is its shade, cut is a stone's proportions and brilliance, and carat is its size and weight. You may have to sacrific one C in favor of the others in order to fit your wallet.

- **Understand her style.** If your bride-to-be wears understated white gold, then a huge rock on a yellow band is probably wrong. If she likes her jewelry flashy, a subdued ring will likely disappoint. Try to match your choice with what she already wears and, clearly, prefers.

- **Stalk her social media channels.** See those rings she's pinning to her Pinterest board? They're aimed at you, dummy.

- **Know her ring size.** Obviously, asking will spoil the surprise, so try to peek in her jewelry box. Failing that, buy larger rather than smaller. It's easier to size down than up.

- **Keep calm and move on.** Don't settle for *a* ring if you think *the* ring is still out there. Keep hunting and pony up your heard-earned money only when you know she'll be happy with what you've bought.

Other Points to Consider

- **It doesn't have to be a diamond . . . or even have a gemstone at all.** The idea of diamonds as the be-all-end-all engagement ring rock is a decades-old marketing ploy. (Not to mention that the diamond industry is involved with some ugly politics, which your future spouse may not wish to support.) Modern synthetic stones are a great alternative—just make sure she knows it's not "real." Other types of gems can make a bold statement (think Princess Diana and the Duchess of Cambridge with that iconic sapphire). Find out whether a particular gemstone has special meaning for her and create a ring with that as the centerpiece. Also popular are complex geometric designs in which the manipulation of the metal is the showstopper.

- **Go handmade . . . or antique.** Many couples are opting for handmade engagement rings and bands. These one-of-a-kind works of art can be purchased from a local craftsperson or just as easily on the Web; visit the online marketplace Etsy and search for "rings" in their Weddings section. For a unique vintage look, shop antiques shops and estate sales. Just be sure your bride-to-be is okay with a "used" ring.

- **To heirloom . . . or not.** The choice to pass down an heirloom can be deeply personal and establish a closer connection between your fiancée and your family. Honoring this tradition is truly special, but don't feel obligated. If you suspect she won't like the family ring, placing the stones in a new setting or on a new band can strike a balance.

Popping the Question

Each couple has a few moments that you will remember for the rest of your married lives: The birth of your first child. Your purchase of a family home. That time you totally nailed the karaoke chorus of "Rollin' in the Deep." And, of course, the moment you proposed. So don't blow it!

Before you do it, consider these points:

- **Make it personal.** Time, place, and setting all matter. Choose something tied to your relationship, like the site of your first date or your favorite outdoor location. The moment will be that much more memorable. Also, time it so that you have a little breathing room before and after; the day of a big trip, event, or work obligation is probably not the wisest choice.

- **Keep it private.** Public proposals seem like a cute idea and make great YouTube videos, but unless (1) you're sure she'll say yes and (2) the place has special meaning to the two of you, all a public proposal does is put her on the spot and make you look like an attention grabber. Remember, a proposal is not a stunt.

- **Consider asking her parents' permission.** Bucking tradition is fine, but some consider traditions like this one to be an important gesture of respect. If your fiancée and her family fall into this category, ask for her parents' blessing. They'll love you for it.

- **Think of hiring a secret photographer.** This idea is not for everyone, so use your judgment to decide whether your potential bride would love this kind of surprise. For the right couples, it's a great way to capture that sweet moment when she realizes what's happening, and her face changes into that beautiful look between a smile and tears.

- **Don't steal another couple's thunder.** Romance is in the air, you're both dressed up, music is playing . . . but it's not for you. Proposing at another couple's wedding is tacky at worst and disastrous at best. Give your fiancée-to-be the solo spotlight she deserves.

- **Start by setting the mood.** Not necessarily soft music and candles (unless that's your thing), just choose an environment you know she'll feel comfortable in. (Don't forget: she'll likely start to cry.)

- **Be sure you have the ring ready.** Put it someplace secure (check pockets for holes) and easily accessible. Trust us: losing the ring will ruin your day.

- **Get down on one knee.** It's hard to go wrong with tradition here. This simple gesture tells her you're giving yourself to her.

- **Keep it short but heartfelt.** Practice in the mirror beforehand if you're worried you'll mess up. Once you go down on that knee, she'll know. Don't make her wait!

Six Questions Everyone's Going to Start Asking You

If you're not the long-suffering type, here's some bad news: you're about to get peppered with the same questions over and over and over again. Better have the proper answers at the ready.

1. **"How did you propose?"**
   Be prepared to tell this story to everyone and anyone except maybe your buddies, who won't really care how you did it as long as they're invited to the wedding.

2. **"When's the big day?"**
   Would it kill these people to wait until they get an invitation? Don't worry about specifics; a vague "next fall" will do until you've nailed down a date.

3. **"Are you inviting so-and-so?"**
   Awkward. This question always runs the risk of opening a Pandora's box of personal politics, but be ready for it. Because you will get asked, especially by nosy family members.

4. **"How did the two of you meet?"**
   If you're lucky, this one will be asked while your fiancée is at your side. Let her tell the story, for the umpteenth time.

5. **"What did [insert ex-girlfriend's name] say when she found out?"**
   Really awkward. Rest assured that more than a few people will be tactless enough to ask it. Politely say you're not concerned about your ex's reaction and then move on to another topic.

6. **"Are you nervous?"**
   The stereotype is that women are excited about the wedding and men are nervous. You're not nervous. You have this book.

The Name Game

Years ago, you got married and your wife took your surname. But it's the twenty-first century, Ward, and she may not want to be known as Mrs. Cleaver. If your future spouse is more traditional and readily chooses to give up her last name, the question is moot. But if she's not sure, here's how to figure out the decision—together.

- **Talk honestly talk about it.** If you'd like her to take your name, tell her so. Don't pressure or guilt her, and certainly don't imply that this is a test of whether she loves you. Just make sure she knows how you feel.

- **Think about the consequences.** Perhaps your fiancée has built a thriving career and is concerned a name change will diminish her hard-earned cred. Perhaps she doesn't like your last name (no offense, dude) or simply likes her own name. She's had it all her life, after all. However, even if her legal last name matches yours, she can continue to use her unmarried name professionally (or in her e-mail address or wherever). In any case, remember: she's the one who has to deal with all the paperwork and red tape a name change entails—changing her Social Security card, driver's license, bank accounts, work-related human resources paperwork, voter registration, and more.

- **Consider hyphenation.** Joining both surnames with a hyphen is a legitimate choice for those who want the best of both worlds, especially for women who have built a strong career before marriage. A husband can take his spouse's name, too, so don't be shy about offering to do so if you want. Keep in mind that in most places you'll need a court order to officially change your name and that you'll likely see butchered names in paperwork and anything that uses an outdated computer system.

Ten Things That Are Definitely Going to Change after Marriage

Marriage is more than an expensive ring and a joint income tax return. It's a transformation from you to two. Here are ten things that are going to change after marriage (and we promise, no more bad rhymes).

1. **Your health.** This will matter to someone other than you and your mom, so take care of yourself.

2. **Your money management.** You are now spending (and saving) for two.

3. **Your relationships.** Other women are no longer "possibilities"—obviously.

4. **Your social role.** People, even your old friends, will start seeing you as one half of a pair.

5. **Your relationship with your wife.** It'll be easier to take your partnership for granted, so do your darndest to ensure that doesn't happen.

6. **Your first impression on people.** Others will see you as more mature and, therefore, take you more seriously. Don't question it; let them have their delusions.

7. **Your hopes, goals, and dreams.** You'll still want the same things, but now you're sharing those things with someone else.

8. **Your friendships.** Married couples tend to gravitate toward other married couples and away from single friends. Be prepared.

9. **Your sense of commitment.** Before marriage, it was a work in progress. Now? You've sealed the deal.

10. **Your perception of yourself.** Realizing that your life is intertwined with another's and that you are, in part, responsible for that person's well-being means that your entire outlook will change. That's a big deal.

Five Things That Definitely *Won't* Change after Marriage

Yes, marriage changes *some* things, but as the saying goes, the more things change . . .

1. **You.** You'll still be the same ole you. You'll just see yourself differently.

2. **Your sex life.** If your sex life changes at all, it'll get better.

3. **Your past.** Any guy who thinks marriage is a way to escape the past is fooling himself.

4. **Your finances.** If you were broke going into the wedding, chances are you'll be broke coming out, and vice versa.

5. **Your happiness.** If you're getting married solely to fill a void in your life, you're setting yourself up for failure. Marry your fiancée because you want to spend the rest of your life with her, period.

Wedding Planning Stuff

It's Only One Day: Keeping Perspective

It's going to be one of the biggest days of your life. Thousands, if not tens of thousands, of dollars will be invested in making it the best day possible. Hundreds of moving parts will have to go off without a hitch in order to make it all happen. And scores of people are going to be there watching the whole joyous event unfold.

No pressure, right?

But here's the thing: something inevitably will go wrong. And that's okay. These are a few things to keep in mind so that the pressure of the big day doesn't get to you.

- **Know that you can't control everything.** That's both unreasonable and impossible.

- **Know that if you try to control everything, you will fail.** See above.

- **No wedding is ever perfect.** Everyone has at least one messy episode. One bad thing does not detract from all the good of the day. Years later, that screw-up will make for a great story, so embrace it.

- **Your guests will follow your lead.** If you're happy, they'll be happy. React badly to a situation and so will they.

- **Look around—you're surrounded by hired professionals, close friends, and family members.** If a crisis arises, lean on them to help avert disaster.

- **If a problem is distracting you or your bride from enjoying the moment, delegate damage control to someone else** (such as your best man) and remove yourselves from the situation. Pose for a picture, get down to the Chicken Dance, or sneak outside for a quiet moment together.

- **Most of all, remember that in a few hours you're going to be alone with your new wife.** It will all be worth it.

A Guide to All the People Who Will Help You Pull This Off

Unless you're sneaking off for a quickie ceremony at the town hall or a Vegas chapel officiated by Elvis, it's not an overstatement to say that planning a wedding is like putting together a complex, potentially dangerous machine. Thankfully, you're going to have a lot of help. Trained, professional help. These people will be there for you. Defer to their expertise.

- **Wedding Planner**—There isn't an aspect of putting together a wedding these folks have not done a hundred times before: scouting the venue, ordering flowers, planning the rehearsal dinner, and giving your wedding a stylish "look." Lots of pressure off your back!

- **Day-Of Coordinator**—If you prefer to DIY your arrangements but don't want to spend the big day calling the shots, a day-of coordinator can be a big help when it comes to, well, the day of. She'll do all

the confirming, coordinating, and timeline
management at your wedding location and
rehearsal venue (as opposed to a wedding
planner, who makes *and* executes the plan).

- **Caterer**—Handles the food and sometimes
  the service, too; may be attached to the
  venue or you may hire one individually.
  If you have an all-inclusive package with
  your venue, you're all set. Otherwise, plan
  to pick out a caterer (and the food) months
  ahead of time.

- **Photographer/Videographer**—If you want
  the kind of stunning photos that will take
  your breath away thirty years later, hire
  these folks. Be sure your photo pros have
  the right kind of equipment—a built-in
  flash and auto-zoom ain't gonna cut it—and
  make sure you'll receive all images on a
  flash drive or memory card so that you can
  duplicate them as often as you want.

- **Florist**—For all things flowers. You and
  your bride will work closely with a florist
  to decorate according to your wedding's

theme. A florist won't always be necessary; some venues supply their own decorations, and outdoor or destination weddings often let the setting speak for itself.

- **Disc Jockey (DJ)/Band**—Match the music to your wedding's vibe—jazz or classical for a classy affair, a cover band for a rockin' party, electro for an eighties throwback. Be sure to pass on special requests beforehand—and be firm! If you don't want your guests grooving to the Macarena or the Chicken Dance, make those wishes crystal clear to your musical entertainment.

- **Printer**—A good local stationery source will have dozens of ready-made templates for invitations, thank-you notes, and place cards. For a custom look, collaborate with an independent artist; personalized handmade letterpress designs, for example, can be found online (again, try Etsy.com).

- **Hair and Makeup Stylists**—Wedding hair is a BIG DEAL. If your fiancée already has a trusted hairdresser, problem solved; if not, she'll probably be hiring a specialist. Some hair stylists will travel to the wedding location; others will ask the wedding party to go to the salon before dressing up. The same goes for makeup artists.

- **Officiant**—Usually a priest or clergy member (though it doesn't have to be), this person will conduct the ceremony and pronounce you husband and wife. Expect to meet a few times before the big day. If you're tying the knot in a church, you may even need to take marriage classes. Fun!

- **Limo Driver**—If you hire a limo, the driver will be a valuable link in the chain, tasked with delivering you on time and looking great. Reliability is a must—get references.

- **Family and Friends**—Even more than any of the professionals listed above, your family and friends are a valuable resource in helping you organize details, welcome guests, and keep everything under control. Be sure to thank them afterward!

How to Budget for a Wedding

As of the writing of this book, the average wedding in the United States cost about the same as the average new car ($29,000 for the wedding, $31,000 for the car). And these days, many couples pay for their own. Time to budget!

1. First, jot down how much money—i.e., cash—you and your bride have available. (Resist the urge to slap everything on your credit card—you'll regret it later.) All your expenditures will come out of that number.

2. Immediately set aside 10% of your planned budget for unexpected expenses. Because unexpected expenses will arise.

3. Rough out a guest list (see page 46) as early as possible. Many wedding expenses (invitations, food, booze, favors, etc.) will scale up or down depending on the number of attendees.

4. Sit down together and start listing what you need versus what you want. Some

things are essentials—the venue, catering, dress and tux, cake—and these will get priority for your dollars. Some things are not essential—live entertainment, a photographer, a sit-down dinner—but you and your future wife may want to have them; you'll budget for these once you've covered the basics. The extras—a live pyrotechnic display, a five-tiered cake in the shape of Iron Man, elephant rides—should be saved for surplus cash, should you be lucky enough to have any.

5. If you're thinking about hiring a wedding planner, now would be a good time to loop in that person and the related fee. Wedding planners might seem like a frivolous expense, but the money you spend here will almost certainly be saved elsewhere thanks to smart planning and efficiencies.

6. Start making phone calls. Get quotes on the necessary items, starting with your venue. Subtract the quotes from that

big number you wrote down in step 1. (Shrinking fast, isn't it?)

7. If your venue has a list of preferred vendors, try to use them for as many items as possible—you'll probably get a break in price. Remember to ask about special discounts or all-inclusive packages.

8. Don't forget smaller hidden costs, like programs for the ceremony and stamps for the invitations—these add up fast. Also remember to include things like taxes, tips, corkage fees, overtime (for DJs, for example), and cleanup/breakdown costs.

9. Once you've taken care of all the essentials, repeat steps 7 and 8 for everything else.

10. Have any money left? Incredible! Go ahead and pluck some more items from your wish list. If not, it's time to sharpen your scissors to cut where you can: either fewer people or less stuff.

How to Have a Wedding on the (Relatively) Cheap

Not everyone daydreams about that huge, lavish wedding with 700 guests—in the Brazilian rainforest. Even if they do, not many people can afford it. Fortunately, it's easy to come in under budget and still throw a quality party. Follow these guidelines and stash your cash for a cool honeymoon trip, instead.

- **Save on music.** It's easy to put together a wedding playlist and let the tunes take care of themselves. Borrow speakers from a buddy in a band to hook up to your iPod, or rent a PA system—it's still cheaper than hiring a DJ. Build a playlist, time it out, and then delegate a groomsman to set up the equipment and press Play so you can dance your big day away.

- **Save on the venue.** Get creative. In spring or autumn, a reception at a pavilion in a local park can save thousands. A family member with an upscale home might host in the backyard, or your church might have a dinner hall available for a modest price.

- **Save on clothing.** Nix the tux. A less-formal dress code will save you (and your wedding party) plenty, as will a second-hand or inherited wedding dress. (That, of course, will be your bride's decision. Do not attempt to nickel and dime her about her gown—it will not end well.)

- **Save on flowers.** By not having any. It's okay! Alternatively, have friends lend blossoms from the bounty of their garden.

- **Save on food.** A buffet-style reception (instead of a sit-down dinner) can save heaps of cash. Feel free to do the food prep yourself if you or friends can tackle such a big job, or seek out an affordable catering option from a local restaurant. Alternatively, stick to a "cocktail reception" with only snacks and drinks—just keep in mind that guests will eat more hors d'oeuvres (and drink more booze) than they would before a full dinner.

- **Save on photos.** If you really don't need that deluxe photo album, video highlights reel, or keepsake image trinkets, clip them out of your budget. Supplement a bare-bones formal portrait package with candid pics from your guests: set three or four disposable cameras on each table with a note encouraging everyone to snap pictures. Place a box at the exit for folks to deposit the cameras. You'll end up with hundreds of photos—some awful, some hilarious, and some real gems—and will have spent next to nothing.

Location, Location, Location

You're going to get married. You're going to throw a big party. And you're going to invite a load of your closest family and friends. So where're you going to do it?

To Church or Not to Church?

A little over half of U.S. weddings are held in a church. If you want a traditional religious ceremony, check with your chosen church early to learn its rules. Some have restrictions on decorations, readings during the ceremony, and so on. You may also have to submit to premarital counseling with your clergy of choice. If having a faith-based ceremony is not vital, consider other places with sentimental value—hometown reception halls, a favorite vacation spot—or anywhere that's particularly memorable.

Indoors or Out?

Gardens, beaches, and parks can all be excellent places to say "I do"—or they can be disasters. Before deciding to go al fresco, consider the drawbacks of holding your ceremony out in the open: weather can be terrible; guests can get sunburned, dirty, or bug-bitten; strangers may pass by and rubberneck. You might also be limited to a date in the warmer seasons. That said, an outdoor wedding is definitely a refreshing alternative to the standard banquet hall. If you're picking a public space (a beach, say, or a park), be sure to check regulations (will you be able to set up a tent, for example?). If you're opting for a private space (a botanic garden, a hotel courtyard), try to arrange a rain location, just in case. And don't forget to consider the time of day and angle of the sun—you don't want to have to squint to see your beautiful bride.

Do a Destination?

An extravagant, fun, and usually expensive choice, a destination wedding in an exotic location can be amazing, but keep in mind that it will also alienate some guests without the means to attend. If you opt for the white-sand beach or mountain getaway, consider a second, smaller reception for all the local friends and family who couldn't make the big trip.

Where's the Party?

A good reception venue should be big enough to fit all your guests. (Note: not everyone invited to the wedding has to be included at the reception; it's separate from the ceremony.) It should also have clear areas where you can set up food, drinks, and dancing.

Many couples find it easiest to hold the reception at the same location as the ceremony (the social hall of a church, for example, or the ballroom of a hotel), but couples going for a quirky wedding or marrying on a budget may opt for a general gathering place—the local VFW or Elks Club, or even a backyard. These more casual locations can be a blast, but keep in mind that they are a lot more work for you as a couple.

Consider, too, whether you want your reception venue to provide all the party goods (catering, DJ, etc.) or whether you want to supply your own. Also, if the ceremony will be in a different location from the reception, be mindful of distance: out-of-town guests might find navigating local back roads to be a nightmare, so provide clear directions and maps (and remember to arrange logistics like parking, adequate bathrooms, and so on—all things we take for granted with traditional venues).

How to Write a Guest List

You've set a date. You've chosen a venue. You're even pretty sure your future wife isn't going to back out at the last minute. Now for that vexing problem all couples grapple with: the guest list. Thankfully, making one is pretty easy.

1. Create a master list of everyone who must be invited and those you'd like to come. You've chosen a venue, so you should have a basic idea of a final head count. Ignore it. Omit no one from this master list, no matter how remote the possibility that they will attend.

2. Separate the "must attends" (parents, best friends, etc.) and the "would like to attends" (old college friends, coworkers, friends, your parents, etc.).

3. Divide each list in step 2 into people who live nearby and those who will need to travel.

4. About 8 to 10 weeks before the wedding, send an invitation to all the "must attends," no matter how far away they live from the wedding venue.

5. Prioritize the "would like to attends" and then send out invitations until you have reached your desired wedding size. Keep tabs on your RSVPs and hold on to the names that didn't make the cut!

6. As RSVPs come back, you'll find out how many people can't make it. Fill in those gaps with the "would like to attends" who didn't make the initial cut. The closer to the wedding date you are, the more you should pluck from the "those who live nearby" list.

A few more things to keep in mind:

- About 75% to 90% of local invitees will attend.

- Among out-of-town family, about 75% to 80% will attend.

- For out-of-town friends, old college buddies, etc., only about half will be able to make it.

- It's okay to over-invite by about 10%, but the smaller your venue, the more conservative you should be.

How to Make a Seating Chart

Think you've safely navigated the dangerous waters of the "Who Have I Offended This Time?" sea by putting together a complaint-free guest list? Hah! How naive. Now comes the tricky part: arranging them. Here are some tips to get everyone sitting pretty.

- **Find out how many people per table.** Find out from your venue staff how many guests will be seated per table.

- **Get a room layout.** Most venues will have printed floor plans showing where tables will be placed. Ask for one.

- **Decide on a head table.** Will you have a "Sweetheart Table" at the head of the room that seats just the two of you, or a larger table with the entire wedding party?

- **Place parents and siblings first.** This will set the tone for the rest of the seating layout. Some couples divide the room by families. Others commingle families and keep friends separate. Start with the parents and take it from there.

- **Understand family dynamics.** If your families get along, blending the seating is encouraged. If not, split the room in two and let them keep their uneasy distance.

- **Friends next, then distant relatives.** Your relatives may be related by blood, but the family you choose—your friends—are an everyday part of your life. They take priority.

- **Brush up on personality clashes.** To ensure wedding day tensions are kept to a minimum, know ahead of time who is oil and who is water, and seat them accordingly. Ex-spouses who had a bitter breakup should be at different tables (even if they're your parents). Don't plunk one at the back of the room, though; you'll be setting up an argument if you do.

- **Keep friends together.** Sure, you're sharing friends now, but your wife's college buddies and your old camp friends haven't seen each other in years. Let them hang out together.

- **Don't fear the singles table.** It's become a rom-com cliché for a reason: seating unmarried friends and relatives together lets them mingle with alluring strangers. You never know, you might even end up a matchmaker!

- **Don't overthink it.** When all is said and done, if folks doesn't like where they are sitting, they can just deal with it—they're adults. Besides, most people will be up mingling for most of the reception, so once the party starts, seating becomes much less of a big deal.

How to Choose the *Best* Best Man

If you think the president has it hard picking a second-in-command, you haven't dealt with the personal politics of choosing a best man. If you're lucky, your choice will be immediate and obvious. Otherwise, here's how to make the nomination.

- **Your best man should be an active part of your life.** Don't rely solely on sentiment—your childhood best friend may have known you the longest, but that doesn't mean he's the best man for the job. Look to the future, too: a buddy from college may not be a great choice if your lives are already going in separate directions.

- **The best man is a position of responsibility.** He makes the toast, holds on to the ring, and helps with day-of wedding duties. Choose someone reliable and nearby—it'll be hard for him to help if he's on the other side of the country. Also, the best man is traditionally tasked with setting up the bachelor party, so consider the kind of trouble your choice might get you into.

- **The best man is also a social position.** In addition to the toast, he will be doing a lot of meeting and greeting. A wallflower may not be up to the challenge (and you don't want to put him in an uncomfortable position).

- **Yes, you can choose two best men**—for example, if you have two brothers and don't want to pick between them.

- **Family members may pressure you to choose someone specific,** but if their man of choice is going to cause distress on your wedding day—or you just want to pick someone else—you'll have to steel yourself and ignore their wishes.

- **When in doubt, go with a male family member:** your dad, your brother, a close cousin. After all, weddings are about family. Plus, you'll avoid having to choose between friends.

- **Don't forget about groomsmen!** Your wedding party is a great chance to include plenty of your buddies who aren't quite best man material.

When all else fails, remember this old wisdom: a good friend will help you move, but a true friend will help you move a body.

Wedding Bands 101

Remember when you nearly pulled your hair out trying to pick the perfect engagement ring? Yeah, about that: engagement rings are, sorry to say, only the first band of gold (or platinum, or silver, or ore forged in the fires of Mount Doom) that you'll have to deal with. You still need wedding bands, those little bits of jewelry that tell the world you are officially hitched—and yes, chief, you're getting one, too. But shopping for bands has two major advantages: you can definitely take along your future wife, and they're way cheaper than engagement rings. Here's the lowdown.

- **Always view rings with your fiancée.** You both need to be happy with this decision!

- **Start looking at least six weeks before the wedding date,** but earlier is always better.

- **Your fiancée might want to pick out your band,** which is a sweet and symbolic gesture. But remember: you're the one who's going to be wearing it.

- **Consider buying from the same jeweler who sold you the engagement ring.** They're likely to have matching bands, and it'll be nice for your wife to have a matched set.

- **Know what you like.** Not just color, but also style. Plain and unadorned? Inset with jewels? Etched with ancient elven runes? Remember, your ring does not have to match hers. It can, of course, but the choice varies from couple to couple.

- **Consider your lifestyle.** If you do a lot of rock climbing or emergency surgeries on the subway, you probably want something simple and unobtrusive.

- **If you're getting jewels, reacquaint yourself with the four Cs:** clarity (how clear a stone is), color (the shade of the stone), cut (a stone's proportions and brilliance), and carat (the size and weight). These will impact the quality of the stone and, hence, how much the band will cost you.

- If you wear jewelry, match what you typically wear.

- **Don't fear originality.** Tradition's all well and good, but you'll be wearing this ring for the rest of your life.

How to Pick the Perfect Tux

They're not just for James Bond and senior proms—at a black-tie wedding, the tux is it. But let's face it: few men enjoy picking one out. Letting your fiancée choose for you is certainly the path of least resistance, but being the best groom you can be means being man enough to have a say in what you'll wear. Here's how to look sharp.

- **Consider the occasion.** Do you even need a tux? A tuxedo is traditionally worn only after 6 p.m. Morning or afternoon weddings call for a morning suit, usually dark gray, which you can pick up from a menswear store. Don't stifle yourself—for an outdoor or destination wedding, you might be better off with a more lightweight fabric and casual style.

- **Consider your budget.** Groomsmen traditionally foot the bill for their own getups, so be considerate and think about everybody's price range, not just your own. Ultimately, you should aim to get everyone outfitted without breaking the bank.

- **Rent or buy?** Renting is cheaper (usually costing about $70–$175, as opposed to at least $500 to buy) and more easily ensures that your groomsmen will all match. But if you plan to attend a few black-tie events in your life (and don't intend to gain weight), a custom-fit tux is well worth the investment. (See box, page 61.)

- **Feel the right fit.** When your arms are at your sides, your fingertips should reach the bottom of the jacket. Your pants should hit the tops of your shoes with a single "break," or crease at the ankle. And make sure your shirt fits well; you're going to be dancing at the reception and don't want it to turn into a puffy mess when you de-jacket.

- **Rock the bow.** If you're wearing a tux, always go with the bow tie—it's the classic option. Cashmere, wool, and flannel are for winter; in the summer, silk.

- **To 'bund or not to 'bund?** Modern cummerbunds are sleeker and more flattering than their bulky 1970s predecessors, so don't avoid one just because you're having high school flashbacks. A slim sash around the waist actually elongates your silhouette.

- **Beware the trends.** If you're buying, go with classic and traditional (read: black) rather than the latest look (read: blue, velvet, or anything with ruffles). They're called classic for a reason. Fifty years from now, you'll look back on your photos with pride.

- **Keep your fiancée in the loop.** Whether she has a vision for your outfit or has no opinions on your getup, she'll appreciate your thoughtfulness. Hell, if she knows exactly what she wants you to wear, just let her pick it!

If You're Renting: Ask around and research online reviews for a good tux-rental shop well in advance of the wedding. Allow adequate time to comparison shop and get the best fit. If you and your groomsmen are all renting, choose a national chain that can arrange fittings for every guy in the comfort of his own hometown.

If You're Buying: As above—research the shop to make sure the staff is knowledgeable and will help you get the best fit. A good salesperson will be invested in finding the best tux possible for you and your budget. If you're looking to get several wears out of your ensemble, ask for a style that you can pair with alternate shirts, ties, etc., for a variety of occasions.

See a tailor. To avoid the dreaded box-jacket look, have your tux fitted by a professional. Stores and rental shops will likely have one on-site. Keep in mind that alterations can take anywhere from 3 to 6 weeks, so don't delay.

A Head-to-Toe Glossary of Tuxedo Terms

Jackets

- **Classic jacket:** A jacket that looks, well, classic—a full, traditional cut that doesn't hit too close to the torso.

- **Modern-cut jacket:** A slightly trimmer look, with higher armholes that let you move more easily.

- **Slim jacket:** A jacket that's—you guessed it—the slimmest cut of the bunch, with fitted sleeves and a tighter fit around the ribs and chest.

- **Single-breasted jacket:** One column of up to three buttons. Short guys should pick a low button stance (buttons that are closer to the hem).

- **Double-breasted jacket:** Two columns of up to three buttons each. Great for tall and thin grooms who want a wider silhouette; not a good option for shorter or more muscular guys.

- **Notched lapel:** The least formal lapel style, with a triangular space where the collar meets the lapel.

- **Peaked lapel:** V-shaped lapels that lie just outside the collar line.

- **Shawl collar:** A smooth, curved lapel. This notch-free option is best for muscular or stocky guys.

- **Lining:** The material on the inside of the jacket. A lighter-weight lining is best for warm weather (duh), a heavier weight in colder temps. A "canvassed" lining is the best bet—it'll help the jacket's shape stay sharp (the alternative, "fused" lining, is more likely to bubble). Colors and patterns are up to you; keep them basic for maximum re-wearability.

Waistcoat or Vest

- Worn under the jacket, a good alternative to cummerbunds for bigger guys. Can be formal or casual, depending on the wedding's mood or theme.

Shirts

- **Fly placket:** A buttonless shirtfront. If your shirt has studs (instead of buttons), the studs should match your cufflinks.

- **Wing collar:** The conventional tuxedo collar. Stands around the neck, with pressed downward points at the front.

- **Banded collar:** Also called a mandarin collar, this rounded collar can be worn sans tie.

- **Laydown collar:** This collar looks almost identical to your average dress shirt collar—folds over at the neck, a wide division between points.

- **French cuffs:** Sleeve cuffs that fold over and stay closed with cufflinks. The classic option for formalwear (and a great opportunity to rock some cool man-jewelry).

Regarding Gift Registries

The wedding registry, aka a cheat sheet for gift givers, is a list of household goods you make with your future wife that your guests will buy for you. It's not a list of demands—you're not Bridezilla and Groomzilla, after all—but it is a wish list, so it's important to assemble it with thought and care. Here's how.

- **Register early.** Don't delay—sign up with your chosen retailers before you start sending out invitations.

- **Pick the right stores.** Make sure your retailer of choice has a wide selection and is easy to access nation- and even world-wide. Online registries are great, but an offline version will be helpful for your less technologically inclined relatives. You may love Fancy Mart, but if Great-Aunt Susan can't easily find what you're registered for, all you're doing is excluding her from the gift-giving fun.

- **Make more than one.** Registries at mul-tiple retailers (between two and five) give people options. And options are good! But be careful not to register for the same item at different stores; you don't want to end up with six blenders.

- **Know your needs and wants.** Your first priority are needs, then add the wants. (Be realistic: if that bread maker is going to sit in the box, don't add it to the list.)

- **Upgrade your current stuff.** Don't hesitate to register for better versions of things you already own. Now is the time to get your hands on a full set of matching knives and forks, glassware, or dinner plates.

- **Pick a pattern.** A matching set of fancy china is one of the most traditional wedding registry gifts there is. Your bride will likely have a look in mind, so let her steer the decision, and only veto if you really, really hate it (they're just plates, after all).

- **Over-register.** A large list gives people options, and options are good—especially when it comes to price range. Be sure to include affordable items (like a nice set of tea towels) with your crystal punch bowls and Japanese steak knives.

- **Check return policies.** Double gifts, last-minute changes, and so on. Things happen. Make sure you can return registry items.

- **Gift cards are okay.** Some gift givers prefer them, and as newlyweds you're going to have unexpected expenses. Gift cards will be welcome at those times.

- **Say thank you.** We don't even need to list this, right? (See page 130 for tips.)

Regarding Religious Traditions

For many couples, weddings have a significance that goes beyond the union of two people—they have a spiritual and religious component, too. Here's how to incorporate traditions in good faith.

- **The decision to recognize religious traditions belongs to you and your bride alone.** However, for the sake of peace and unity, it's wise to allow immediate family to have some say. If you are nonreligious or an atheist, consider including a nod to their wishes in the ceremony—maybe a short biblical reading or a piece of religious music. You're not betraying yourself by allowing a small gesture that will make family happy.

- **By the same token, it's okay to refuse any religious acknowledgment if you feel your principles don't allow it.** Just be prepared to deal with the potential fallout.

- **If you and your bride have differing religions, wedding planning can be tricky but not impossible.** Some couples have separate ceremonies, one for each set of beliefs. The easier and more common approach is to recognize both beliefs on the same day with a blended ceremony. You may need to shop around for officiants (and venues), but combining traditions is a common and joyful way to bring families together.

- **Remind anyone critical of your choices that the wedding is about you and your bride.** But do so politely, with a smile and a thank you, and walk away if an argument is brewing. Nothing good comes from debating religion on your wedding day!

- **No matter what, stand together as a couple.** If family is battling you on the topic, no matter whose family it is, show a united front.

How to Choose an Officiant

That person who asks if you take this woman and lets you kiss her? That's the wedding officiant. Seems like an easy enough job—so easy that many people don't put much thought into choosing one. But it's a choice that deserves some consideration. Here's what to keep in mind.

- **The officiant sets the tone for the ceremony.** Choose someone whose personality fits well with yours.

- **If you and your fiancée are members of the same church or synagogue or temple, etc., and plan to get married there, great.** You're familiar with the same clergy members and presumably you like them. Similarly, if you or your future wife maintains a strong bond with a childhood religious leader—and you're planning a hometown wedding—now's the time to call that person into service.

- **Some officiants come with the venue, so to speak.** If you must get married in that adorable little church by the sea, be prepared to get married by the kooky little priest who lives there, too.

- **Some religious officiants will marry you only in their church.** Others are willing to travel. If you find someone you like, be sure to ask how flexible he or she is on this point.

- **Secular officiants are easy to find.** Contact your county clerk's office for local justices of the peace or use the Internet to your advantage. Treat this search just as you would a search for a caterer: interview people, get prices, vet their performance. You're paying for a service, after all, so make sure it's good.

  Friends and relatives can be ordained through the Universal Life Church, allowing them to perform wedding ceremonies (just be sure to verify that this practice is recognized by your state). But consider carefully before asking your buddy to preside over the proceedings: you want someone who is close to you and can take the duty seriously.

- **Once you've found a good candidate, don't be afraid to ask questions.** Are custom vows allowed? Are your faiths (or lack thereof) a problem? Are you required to attend premarital classes? Are you expected to pay for travel if you're getting married far away?

How to Write Your Own Vows

Back when tradition ruled the day, couples would recite a pretty standard "to have and to hold" set of vows, and that was that. These days, couples like to be more involved in the process. They want something specific to themselves and their relationship—and that's cool. Just keep these tips in mind.

- **Ask first.** Some officiants and houses of worship won't allow custom vows. Bummer—but better to know before you invest a lot of time into crafting a speech.

- **Talk to each other.** What do you each want from the other? Knowing what you expect from your life together will spark ideas. Also, talk about the tone you'd like to set. Poetic and loving? Funny and witty? Utterly irreverent? All are fine, just decide before you start writing. You don't want her making a heartfelt poetic speech about your partnership while yours is loaded with jokes and puns.

- **Give yourself time.** This is the most important day of your life—you don't want your vows to be a zero-hour rush job. Write early and often, making a few drafts if you need to.

- **Express yourself.** If you're going to do custom vows, make them count. Include something that is unique to you or your relationship. And don't feel like you have to get all highfalutin—something as simple as a list of everything you love about your bride-to-be can be truly meaningful.

- **Steal.** Pablo Picasso said, "Good artists copy; great artists steal." If you hear a fantastic line at another wedding, in a movie, wherever, take it! Just don't get too obvious with your references, else you'll risk sounding tacky (no "you had me at hello" kind of stuff).

- **Consider the length.** You may have a lot to say, but resist the urge to go on too long. You don't realize just how long 30 seconds is until you're standing in front of a crowd of two hundred people.

- **Say them aloud.** Writers often read their prose out loud to ensure it sounds okay. Since you really will be uttering these vows on your wedding day, it's best to try them out beforehand to ensure they sound as good as they read. Practice speaking slowly—seriously, it's amazing how easy it is to rush when you're nervous.

- **Print them out.** It's okay to keep a hard copy of your vows tucked in your tux jacket on the big day. (Because, really, you've got too many other things on your mind to memorize.) Print the vows in a font large enough to read, and leave plenty of space between lines.

Wedding Food (and Drink) 101

Everyone loves tasty little bacon-wrapped scallops, tiny hot dogs, and classed-up tater tots, but wedding food is more than just snacks. It's a way of being kind to the friends and family who have all shown up to see you cry manfully as you marry the woman of your dreams. Your bride-to-be probably has plenty of ideas for how to feed everyone, but here's a breakdown of the options.

• **Cocktail Reception**—A few cocktails, some hors d'oeuvres, and the company of a small group of close-knit friends and family. Catering these is inexpensive, and it's easy to DIY. Just be sure to specify this kind of reception on your invitations so that expectations are properly set (i.e., no one arrives too hungry).

   Good for: Keeping it casual (and cheap!)

• **Afternoon Luncheon**—A good option for early-in-the-day weddings and especially for DIY weddings. An assortment of salads, cold and hot pasta dishes, and sandwiches makes this one easy.

Good for: Receptions in places like parks, the beach, a barn, and so on

- **Catered Buffet**—A catered spread means no need for servers (though you can opt for people to work the buffet) and a fairly easy setup. Prices can range from highly affordable for an assortment of food trays to deluxe packages that include servers, dinnerware, and so on. "Make-your-own" bars—where guests doctor up their dishes— are a popular option.

  Good for: DIY or smaller weddings

- **Sit-Down Dinner**—A formal dinner usually provided by servers, this is the traditional option for most weddings. Guests typically choose from several (albeit limited) menu options when sending in their RSVP. Some venues provide their own caterer; with others, you'll have to hire a caterer separately.

  Good for: Bigger weddings (no crowded buffet lines!)

- **Dessert Only**—Just what it sounds like: nothing but sweets and treats (and cocktails, should you choose). Surround your traditional cake with good stuff like pies, cookies, or even a candy buffet. Remember to be sensitive to guests keeping to low-sugar diets (a token bowl of mixed nuts or something savory will do).

  Good for: Evening weddings (and chocoholics)

- **Food Stations**—A themed twist on a buffet, this will cost you some money but will be memorable. A series of stations offering differing styles of cuisines: sushi over here, BBQ over there, Italian this way, etc. Note that not all venues can accommodate this kind of setup.

  Good for: Foodies and adventurous eaters

- **Open Bar**—The spendiest of all drink options, this allows your guests to drink anything—wine, beer, hard liquor—to their heart's content. A full bar is usually 20% liquor, 15% beer, and 65% wine. Figure one drink per hour per (adult) guest, and scale up from there.

Good for: Gracious couples, or those with sky-high budgets

- **Limited Bar**—Pretty much what it sounds like: guests are limited to certain drinks (wine, beer, and maybe a signature cocktail) and sometimes certain times during the reception. For beer and wine only, stock 20–30% beer and 70–80% wine (adjusting for your crowd's tastes, of course).

  Good for: More cost-conscious couples, or DIY weddings

- **Cash Bar**—Let's be real: no one likes being invited to a wedding only to be forced to fork over dollars for drinks. Sure, you and your bride will save, but your family and friends will probably hate you.

  Good for: Almost nobody—consider a serve-yourself wine and beer bar at the back of the room, or cut costs elsewhere in planning

- **No Bar**—Yes, some people don't drink at weddings—at all. And that's okay! Stock up with plenty of soft drinks, fruity "mocktails," and sparkling cider for a faux-Champagne toast.

  Good for: Couples who are booze-free, for whatever reason (religion, health, etc.)

How to Pick Your Wedding Music

Music is an important part of almost everyone's life. Songs evoke memories and feelings. They take you back to specific times and places. They can make or break your mood. So it goes without saying that choosing the right tunes is a hugely important part of creating the perfect wedding experience. Here's how.

- **For the Ceremony:** Wagner's "Bridal Chorus" (better known as "Here Comes the Bride") is the most important song for the ceremony. Other traditional opening numbers include Pachelbel's "Canon in D," Bach's "Arioso," and Mozart's "Romance (Andante) from Serenade No. 13 for Strings in G Major" (phew). Once the ceremony is in full swing, anything goes: light instrumental music (piano or solo guitar) can help fill in the background, a brief choir number or song by a talented friend, or an all-sing hymn if the ceremony is religious.

Don't forget to pick outro music, too—you need something to walk away to!

- **For Cocktail Hour:** This is a time for mingling and pre-party meeting and greeting, so unobtrusive instrumental music is ideal. Jazz is a great choice, especially if you book a live band. If you want something more modern, try low-key electronic music, post-rock (think Moby, Mogwai, or Air), or even hip-hop instrumentals. Remember to keep the volume low enough that your guests can hear one another talk.

- **For Entering the Reception:** When you and your bride burst through to doors to thunderous applause, you want something upbeat on the speakers—and something that screams you. Geeks might go with the Star Wars Imperial March. Party people may choose "Highway to Hell." Whatever it is, make sure it will energize the crowd— this is the start of the party, after all!

- **For Your First Dance:** This is what will become "your song," so choose one that you, as a couple, will embrace for years to come. Also remember that you're going to be dancing to it in front of a crowd, so keep it short. Under four minutes is a must, under three is ideal. Anything longer will feel like an eternity.

- **For the Reception:** If you're going the DJ route, meet with him or her ahead of time to talk playlists. Name a couple favorite songs (and the ones you absolutely hate), but stick to general genres so that you can step aside on the day of—that's why you hired a human instead of plugging in an iPod. Same goes if you're hiring a band: discuss musical options well in advance so that they'll have time to learn anything not already in their repertoire. When picking your songs, remember the makeup of your crowd. Keep it PG-13 at most, vary genres (no one wants to hear three straight hours of power ballads), and be sure to have at least a few songs to please everyone. There should be at least five opportunities to slow dance, and the night should close with a slow number, but mix in a lot of upbeat stuff, too, to keep people excited. Otherwise, rock it the way you, your friends, and your families like to rock it. There are no wrong choices here.

How to Give Your Mom (and Your Fiancée's Mom) Her Say

Your wedding is a big deal for you and your future wife . . . and for your mothers, too. They're closing the doors on big chapters of their lives, watching their offspring become true adults, and that is no small thing for a mother. Here's how to keep them happy.

Handling Your Mom

1. From the start, make sure she knows that you and your fiancée have things under control (even if you, uh, don't, exactly). Projecting competence and confidence will help forestall any well-meaning yet unwelcome meddling on her part.

2. Be willing to listen to her input. Listening doesn't mean that you have to act on what she says, and sometimes all Mom wants to know is that she's being heard.

3. Seek her input on a small matter to make her feel like she's contributing. Something minor but noticeable, such as what song to play during your reception entrance or how to honor your grandparents.

4. Include her in the girls-only events. Suggest that she go dress shopping with your fiancée (but only if your fiancée agrees!). Your mother will feel like part of the process, even if the dress decision truly belongs to your lady.

5. Ask her to offer a surprise from you at the bridal shower—maybe a funny and romantic video you made, or a small matching gift for her and your bride. She'll be delighted to do something for her son and play a visible role in the celebration.

Handling Your Fiancée's Mom

1. As with your own mother, from the very start ensure that she knows everything is under control. Well-intended meddling is still meddling.

2. Always defer to your fiancée's judgment when it comes to her own mother. She's had years to get to know all her maternal weaknesses and quirks, and you do not want to get in a fight with your future mother-in-law before you've even tied the knot. Trust me.

3. Allow her to make a decision about something related to the wedding, preferably concerning her daughter and ideally something neither you nor your fiancée consider vital. Perhaps she can pick the song for the father/daughter dance or choose the table settings. Give her the chance to offer input without running the whole show.

4. If you're doing custom wedding favors or "welcome bags," have your mother-in-law plan and host a preparation party during which the bridal party gets together and assembles the packages.

5. If you know she'll have a specific demand— wanting your bride to wear a family

heirloom, for instance—talk it over with your fiancée. If the expected demand is no big deal to you, accept your future mother-in-law's input, just be sure it doesn't open the door to further demands.

How to Survive Your Bachelor Party

The bachelor party is one of the most celebrated—and controversial—parts of the modern engagement tradition. They are often the stuff of legend. Entire movies have been made about them. But even though you want to have fun, you don't want to ruin your marriage before it even starts. Here's how to make it through the minefield with nothing worse than a hangover.

- **Share your preferences.** If you chose your best man wisely (page 52), he will not now lead you into a den of debauchery. If you want a night of bar-hopping, tell him so that he can arrange for safe transportation. If you prefer an afternoon with the guys at a ballgame, or even a night of hardcore video gaming, say so. Remember, it's your celebration.

- **If you don't like *those* clubs, speak up.** Strip joints are by no means a requirement for your last hurrah. Let your best man know that you don't want that kind of a bachelor party. Believe us, that feeling is more common than you think.

- **Avoid the night before.** At one time, bachelor parties were commonly held the night before the wedding. This is a bad idea for obvious reasons. You don't need to be bleary-eyed on your wedding day!

- **Download a drunk dial app.** Even better, leave your phone at home and take along a burner instead in case you need to call 911. No good can come of the calls and texts you'll make on the night of your bachelor party.

- **Know your circle of friends.** If you're surrounded by the sort of people who will egg you on to do things you shouldn't do, suggest safe, sane options before the party is planned.

- **No need to prove yourself.** You don't need to prove how much you can drink, how many numbers you can get, or that you can totally do that wild stunt if someone will just hold your beer. This is about enjoying a last night as an unmarried man, not about proving something to dudes you should be long past needing to prove anything to.

Ten Things to Do the Night Before

Wow, is it here already? It's ridiculous that it got here so fast. But here you are, staring into the Abyss of Impending Matrimony. Time to tie up a few loose ends.

1. **Turn off the computer.** No Facebook or Twitter or social media. Tune out and focus on tomorrow.

2. **Hang out—calmly.** Spend some quiet time with your bride or buddies. No partying, just talking.

3. **Eat light.** You want to be able to fit into your tux.

4. **Drink light.** If you're drinking the night before, keep it under control. Wedding day hangovers suck.

5. **Read your vows.** And then read them again. Practice makes perfect.

6. **Lay out your things.** Prepare now and tomorrow will be easier.

7. **Prepare a surprise.** A love note or little gift to give to your bride tomorrow.

8. **Delegate tasks.** Let your best man take care of minor last-minute issues.

9. **Reminisce.** You're actually going to marry that girl tomorrow. Awesome. Take a moment to reflect on that.

10. **Sleep.** A lot of grooms pull all-nighters, much to their regret. Don't.

Wedding Day
Stuff

How to Melt Cold Feet

There is no denying it: this is a big day. So big that it wouldn't be altogether surprising if you got wedding day jitters. Hey, it happens. Even the most laid back guy can turn into a wreck once the reality of the big day starts to settle in. But you've got to keep it together, man! Here's what to do.

- **Know what's getting to you**. If you can figure out what's giving you the Wedding Day Jitters, you'll have a better chance of getting past them.

- **Look past the crowd.** If being in front of a crowd makes you nervous, try this public speaking trick: look above everyone's heads and concentrate on the back wall of the room. The crowd will stay in your peripheral vision and become an anonymous blob.

- **Talk about it.** You chose your best man to be the head of your support team, so use him for support. Pull him aside and tell him you're nervous. He'll call you an idiot. You'll feel better.

- **Have a drink.** As in, one drink—but only if you're the type who settles down with a single drink. Otherwise, avoid altogether, or opt for an herbal tea or other calming beverage (hey, these things work!).

- **Breathe.** Inhale for four counts, exhale for eight—it's been proven to calm your autonomic nervous system.

- **Stand up straight.** An erect and confident posture will help you exude "groomness" on your wedding day. Stand up straight, pull your shoulders back, and don't fidget.

- **Project confidence.** Make eye contact when speaking with people (including when reciting your vows) and smile. You can do this.

- **Think ahead.** Fact is, this day is going to be over before you know it. Think about how you'll be consummating the marriage later—that part will be awesome—and the next couple of hours will zip by.

Tips for the Well-Groomed Groom

Maybe you're already the dapper type, able to flawlessly execute the aftershave pat while sporting trim nails and an impeccable haircut. In that case, your wedding day prep will probably be like any other day. For the rest of us . . . well, read on.

- **Consider a manicure.** Seriously. Well-tended nails will make you feel more sophisticated. Opt for a simple clip and buff (i.e., no polish) for a clean and natural look.

- **See a tailor.** You did follow the advice on page 58 regarding your tux, didn't you? Didn't you?

- **Whiten those teeth.** Over-the-counter strips are cheap and easy, and they really do work. Use them the week leading up to your wedding day.

- **Tame those eyebrows.** Go ahead, grab the tweezers and do some plucking a night or two before the wedding. Cleaning up strays seems minor but can make a big difference. Just don't go overboard.

- **Trim some nose hair.** Pinch your nose. With a trimmer, trim any hair sticking out. (If it's not outwardly visible, leave it. Nose hair serves a purpose.)

- **Have a good shave.** A few days before your wedding, switch to a fresh razor (best not to do so the day of, to minimize cuts). Shave slowly and use short strokes to help prevent razor burn and nicks. Using a shaving brush will produce a better lather and help lift hairs for a closer, cleaner shave.

- **Get a haircut.** Go to your barber a week in advance. That'll give your new cut time to grow in and look natural while still appearing fresh and neat.

- **Down there.** If you're not already manscaping, this is the time. If you're inexperienced in this area, tread with caution and opt for only basic trimming.

Ten Things Every Groom Needs in His (or His Best Man's) Pocket

You are about to embark upon the Great Crusade, toward which you have striven these many months. The eyes of the world are upon you. The hopes and prayers of marriage-loving people everywhere march with you. We have full confidence in your courage, devotion to duty, and skill in marriage. We will accept nothing less than full victory on your wedding day—with the help of these ten essentials.

☐ **Aspirin**
   It's going to be a long day.

☐ **Cell phone**
   You may need your best man to make an emergency call. Keep the ringer off during the ceremony (please!).

☐ **List of telephone numbers**
   Vendors, drivers, caterers, and wedding pros; wedding night accommodations; taxi service for guests, etc.

☐ **Cash**
Emergencies happen (you mean no one remembered to pay the band?!). Be ready for one.

☐ **Stain remover pen**
Lots of food and drink and an expensive tux. Better safe than sorry.

☐ **Camera**
Your photographer will be taking care of the fancy stuff, but you and/or your best man may want to snap some outlandish candids.

☐ **Breath mints**
You're going to be playing meet and greet all night long. Freshen up.

☐ **Handkerchief**
Whether you're a crier, a sweat-er, or both, you'll wanna have something to sop up those fluids.

☐ **Lip balm**
If you've got a kissy family, you're going to be kissing a lot of cheeks.

☐ **The ring**
If you forget all else on this list, don't forget this!

How to Cry Manfully

Despite what those beer commercials tell you, men cry about more than a poorly cooked steak. If ever there's a time when tears of joy are warranted, this is it. Here's how to let the waterworks go while retaining your manhood.

- **Embrace your joy.** Your eyes are welling up because you can't believe you're actually marrying this amazing woman. Allow yourself to bask in that feeling.

- **Let those tears come.** Tears are brave. Wiping them away before they trickle down your cheek is unbecoming. Let 'em roll!

- **Stay mum.** Avoid talking if your voice is going to crack. Pause for a moment to compose yourself. Man tears are awesome. Squeaky man voice, not so much. If you can, sneak off for a glass of water.

- **Dab, don't rub.** Use your best man's handkerchief (page 101) to gently pat those tears. Rubbing will redden your eyes. Above all, avoid the honking nose-blowing.

- **Allow others to witness it.** The hallmark of a real Man Cry is being unashamed in the presence of others. When people see the happiness streaming down your face, they'll think you're an awesome husband—because you are.

- **Snap out of it.** If you really can't stop sobbing, visualize something totally un-sad to get yourself back in the game.

How to Rock Your Wedding Photos

If you think hiring a good photographer is the beginning and end of your part in the Quest for the Perfect Wedding Photo, think again. You and your lovely bride will need to strut your stuff for the photos to really shine.

- **Know your best side.** Everyone has one (faces aren't symmetrical!). Go through old pictures and see if you can spot yours.

- **Open your mouth.** Sounds odd. It may even feel awkward. But a glimpse of those pearly whites makes a world of difference when you smile. Put the tip of your tongue at the roof of your mouth, right where it meets your front teeth.

- **Smile with your eyes.** Know why fake smiles look fake? Because the faker isn't smiling with their eyes. Practice in the mirror. Also, smiles are nice, but you don't have to fake one the whole time. A few serious shots can make for romantic memories in years to come.

- **Stand up straight.** Your mom was right—
  it does make you look more handsome.
  Pretend there's a string at the crown of your
  head yanking you to attention.

- **Be well groomed.** You did read "Tips for
  the Well-Groomed Groom," right? Oh, just
  go back to page 98 already.

- **Have a friend off-camera.** A witty friend
  or family member chatting and teasing can
  help add some levity and keep you smiling
  throughout a photo shoot.

- **Be yourself.** It's okay to just be you.

- **Ask for candid shots.** You may end up lik-
  ing the photos you didn't know were being
  taken more than the ones you posed for.

- **Take action.** Posing is fine, but consider a
  walk through the garden or a dance on the
  veranda to let the photographer catch you
  and your bride in motion.

- **Use props.** Glasses in hand, bouquets, guys
  with cigars—whatever suits your personality. Props = fun, and they'll help soak up
  some of your nervousness.

How to Meet and Greet All Those Strangers

If you're a natural politician type, this part will come easy. But if you weren't born to press the flesh, we have bad news for you: a not insignificant amount of time on your wedding day will be spent making small talk with people you won't see for another decade or more. You can't avoid it—you're half of the star of the show. Here's how to survive.

1. Some couples have a greeting line on the way into the reception hall during which they offer a personal hello to everyone entering. Do this—it's the perfect way to get all your hi-and-thank-yous over with in one fell swoop.

2. If your better half is the charming one, let her take the lead. Most people are more interested in the bride than you, anyway.

3. A few short phrases to memorize: "Thank you for coming." "We're so glad you could be here." "Enjoy the party!"

4. Circulate early. The cocktail hour is the perfect time to do a quick circuit of the room, saying hello to the aunts and uncles and distant cousins you never see. Everyone will want some of your time. Give it to them early.

5. Remember that you have a built-in excuse to exit a conversation early. You're the groom! "I should really make my way around the room" is always a legitimate reason to move on.

6. If mingling makes you nervous, consider setting up the reception with a "sweetheart table" for you and your bride, and stick close to it. Allow your guests to come to you. (Just understand that they will. In droves.)

7. Have backup. Have your mother with you as you circulate among her side of the family. Let your best man be your wingman one last time as you work the crowd. Or circulate with your wife on your arm so she steals all the attention.

8. Bring a prop. Even something as simple as a drink in hand can offer a much-needed distraction. If you're getting antsy, "I need to go get a refill" offers an instant escape that no one will question.

How to Nail the First Dance

Up and at 'em, champ. You've got a whole banquet hall full of wedding guests to impress. Yeah, dancing's not really your thing, but come on. Did you see your new wife in that gorgeous wedding dress? Face it, Tiger, you just hit the jackpot. Now go dance with her!

1. You'll be standing slightly offset from each other, not toe to toe. (That's so you don't step on her feet, you klutz.)

2. Take her waist with both hands. They can be overlaid at the small of her back, on her hips (though don't you want to get closer?), or with one hand at the small of her back and the other holding her hand—whatever is most comfortable. Her hands will be clasped behind your neck, or she'll put one on your shoulder and one in your hand.

3. Know who leads? You do. No worries, though. Just sway gently back and forth to the music—from your torso, not from your

arms or shoulders (too much arm movement can make your bride feel like she's getting jerked around). Hopefully you picked a good song, one that means something to you and isn't too long.

4. Now, take tiny sliding steps to turn you and your partner in a circle. Make sure you're both stepping in sync: step right, step back, step left, step forward, repeat. Keep your arms relatively stiff, as if your elbows are locked in place.

5. Talk to your bride. Whisper in her ear about how great she looks. Ask if she remembers when you first met.

6. Exit with grace—and try not to trip.

Day-Of Problems That Will Inevitably Arise—and How to Deal

No matter how much you want your wedding day to be perfect, it won't be. Period. End of story. But if you go into it understanding some common problems that may occur, you'll be prepared to weather any storm like a champ.

- **Ceremony hiccups.** Some little aspect of the ceremony is bound to stumble—sometimes literally, in the case of your ring-bearing nephew. Take small glitches with a smile. Remember, this is not a race. If your best man and your wife's maid of honor know the ceremony inside and out—and they should—they can assist in steering things back on course if things veer too far off script.

- **Wardrobe malfunction.** You're probably not used to gallivanting around in formalwear. Neither are your buddies. Your wife may be a classy dresser, but navigating in a wedding dress is harder than calculus. Bring backup clothing and accessories (such as suspenders for you, comfortable shoes for her, safety pins for everybody, etc.) to cover any slipups and split seams.

- **Someone drank too much.** Have your best man (or a family member of the overimbiber) discreetly pull the person outside and keep them occupied until they settle down. Under no circumstances are you obligated to help someone vomit.

- **You drank too much.** Haven't we taught you better than this? Hopefully you picked a good best man to get you away from the open bar, pour you some water, and help you come back down to earth.

- **Things go off schedule.** You can plan your wedding day down to the minute, but that doesn't mean Fate will listen. Build time into the day's schedule to account for slowdowns, and remain patient no matter what happens.

- **Mechanical/electrical problems.** Blown fuses, bum musical equipment, and busted

buttons can put a damper on your day. Ask
your venue staff if a backup plan is in place
for such situations, or delegate your wedding planner to figure it out beforehand.

- **Wedding professional is unprofessional.**
No matter how much you vet them, one of
your wedding professionals may turn out to
be less than likable. If the problem is time
sensitive (the DJ isn't playing the right
songs), politely ask them to shape up. If
it's just annoying (a snarky waiter), make a
note of the behavior to discuss it later with
a supervisor. Best advice for most problems:
grin and bear it. Your wedding day is not
a day to get into a dispute with a vendor
you'll never use again.

- **Clash of the titans.** Personality conflicts
are practically a wedding mainstay. Following the seating chart advice on page 49 will
help minimize this problem, but no plan is
foolproof. Delegate peacemaking duties to a
trusted friend or family member. Don't play
negotiator on your wedding day!

Your Drunk College Friends and You

A wedding is just a big, expensive party—a party filled with the same people you used to raise hell with. If you're not careful, that can spell danger. Don't let it happen to you.

Handling Your Friends

- **Alert the front lines.** Give your wedding planner a heads-up before the reception. Chances are, she has seen worse and has a few tricks up her sleeve. Talk to the bartender, too: a generous tip will ensure he'll cut people off before they get too smashed.

- **Have a heart-to-heart.** Remind your friends that they're mingling with your bride's family. Make sure they understand that their behavior reflects on you.

- **Beware the awkward toast.** If you think one of your buddies is planning a speech that's, say, colorful, make sure to discuss it prereception (and before you've downed a couple beers).

- **Call in the heavy.** If any of your friends need to be reined in, physically restrained, or escorted to the bathroom, it's your best man's job to do it. That's why you picked him.

Handling Yourself

- **Keep your eyes on the prize.** This night isn't about you and your friends, it's about you and your new bride. Don't forget that.

- **Know your limits.** Your buddies may want to push the open bar to its limits. That's their prerogative. Think twice—or thrice—before joining them.

- **Pace yourself.** You don't need to down a full drink after every toast. A sip is fine. Remember, when the night is over, you still have to perform your husbandly duties. Don't drink so much that you get off to a limp start.

- **Work the crowd.** Though you'll want to spend time with your buddies, an entire banquet hall of people wants a few moments with you. Your friends already know how glad you are to have them there. Your aunt Gertie, on the other hand, needs reassurance.

- **Worry less as the night goes on.** Crazy stuff going down at 1 a.m. is way less likely to spoil the evening than a predinner meltdown.

Your Lovely New Wife

Wedding day jitters are normal—yours and hers. See, the thing about getting married is that it's not just about you anymore. Your wedding day will be the first and one of the most important tests of your partnership. Here's how to be a rock for your lovely new wife so her jitters don't ruin her special day.

- **Keep her among family and friends.** Being with those you love the most can be calming on stressful days.

- **Unless there's family drama.** In that case, keep her occupied with things away from the family, and run interference on any annoying relatives who try to bug her. Teamwork!

- **Express your gratitude.** Make sure she knows how much you admire all the hard work she's put in to making this day perfect. Her months of stress really will be worth it when you remind her how great the flowers look or how awesome the cake tastes.

- **Tell her she's beautiful.** Because she is.

- **Steal a quiet moment together.** It's okay to slip out the back door alone. Your guests will be fine without you.

- **Hold her hand.** A small physical gesture when you're making the social rounds can help keep both of you grounded.

- **Get her a favorite drink.** That doesn't mean she should *drink* drink, but a tipple can sometimes take the edge off.

- **Ask her support team to help.** Her maid of honor and bridesmaids are there to help, so ask them to provide needed distractions. That's their raison d'être!

- **Most of all, LOVE HER.** That's all. Distract her with your love. Have her bask in your adoration. Remind her why you fell for her in the first place, and all the day's worries will melt away.

Regarding the Wedding Night

After months of planning and a whirlwind day with family and friends, the event has finally happened. The party's winding down, the limo (or can-trailing JUST MARRIED-mobile) is idling in the drive, and your hotel room awaits. Now it's just you and your new wife.

Your wedding night is something special. Sure, you've been together for a while, you love each other, and you know each know the other as well as two people can. But tonight is different. This is your first night together as husband and wife. (Again, be sure not to overindulge! The most important thing you'll take away from your wedding day are memories—don't drown them out.)

If you planned well, you're retiring to a room well away from any ongoing party. Before you leave the venue, take stock. Are you forgetting anything (wallet, phone, etc.)? A quick sweep is fine, but your best man can look after things in your absence. If the party is headed into the wee hours, don't feel obligated to see it through. In fact, don't. Take a graceful early exit with your wife.

Also, avoid inviting friends back to your wedding suite after the reception—that can only end in an all-nighter with people passed out on your marital bed. If folks want to throw an afterparty, make sure it happens elsewhere. Everyone will understand you need your alone time.

If you can arrange a special surprise—rose petals on the bed, having a warm bath drawn—go for it, but don't worry if you cannot. Your bride will be happy just to be with you. When you finally retire to your room, take time to savor the moment. (You'll need time, anyway. Tuxes and wedding dresses are as difficult to get off as they are to get on.) Look at your new bride. Isn't she beautiful? And now she's your wife!

Lastly, go slow. Allow every moment to take forever. Whether you're unwinding in the hot tub, feeding each other late-night takeout, or making love, allow yourselves a chance to bask in your first hours alone together—because you'll never have this night with her again.

You Really Are Ready for This

If the massive amount of advice offered by this book (and everyone else in your life) has become overwhelming, stop and take a deep breath. If you're pondering all the information on the previous pages and think there is no way you'll remember it all, then just set that thought aside.

You are ready for this.

Lesser men than you have made it through wedding days more complicated than yours. Seriously. In the United States alone, over 2.5 million guys every year manage to plan and execute one of these celebrations. You really are not alone (but you probably already knew that, if you've being trying to find an available weekend at your chosen venue).

But wedding industrial complex aside, here's the real reason you're ready for this: you were smart enough to read this book. Which means that you're taking an active role in making your wedding day the best day possible. That gives you a major advantage over many—if not most—of those other 2.5 million grooms out there. Best of all, you have an amazing fiancée who is going to be by your side the whole time. And that's a big deal.

After-Wedding Stuff

Read This Stuff Before the Wedding

You've done it! You made it through your big day (relatively) unscathed. Only a few people are mad at you for that embarrassing reception incident. (The less said about that, the better.) You even managed to keep your mother and mother-in-law from fighting. You are officially a married man.

Now the real work begins.

The following sections are intended to get you off to a good start. From little "rules" you didn't think of before marriage to the small courtesies that help a union thrive, these tips will ensure your early days together are good days. After all, if you did all that preparation for just one day of your life, doesn't it stand to reason that you should prepare for all those other days to come?

So don't wait until you're married. Read this section now, before your wedding day, so that you know what to expect. Then when you're done, go get yourself a copy of *Stuff Every Husband Should Know*. You're going to need it!

How to Plan (and Budget for) a Honeymoon

Traditionally, the bride and groom are married in front of all their friends and family, and then in the morning they slip away to a destination as far from those friends and family as they can get (and afford). Mixed messages much? In any case, honeymoon planning is a part of the whole "getting married" thing that sometimes slips through the cracks (or ends up being more expensive than you ever could've imagined). Here's how to make sure that doesn't happen.

Planning

- **Know what you both love.** Whether it's biking through the countryside, lounging on the beach, dancing all night long, or visiting cool microbreweries, make sure you choose a destination you've both wanted to visit and now can explore together. Your shared passions should inform your choice.

- **Consider a travel agent.** Sure, these days it's easy to book things yourself, but a travel agent can remove a lot of the work and stress. Share your budget and your general likes and dislikes (beaches, solitude, active night life, etc.), and most good agents can set up a wonderful trip in no time.

- **Go all-inclusive.** Another way to ease the stress, these packages let you relax knowing your meals, maybe your drinks, and some entertainment are included with your stay.

- **Book well in advance.** This not only saves you money, it will make all the planning that follows so much easier.

Budgeting

- **Know how much you can afford.** Determine the upper limit of all expenses from start to finish. The average honeymoon (seven days, six nights) costs just over $5,000 per couple: budget roughly $700 each for airline tickets, $150–250 for each night in a hotel ($150–$400 if it's all-inclusive), $150 per day for meals, and $300 per day for sightseeing, taxis, souvenirs, and other incidentals. It all can be done for less (or more), but use these numbers as a guideline.

- **Get quotes based on your honeymoon plan.** First, account for major expenses: travel (airfare, gas, etc.), room/resort, car rentals, event tickets, and the like.

- **Calculate meal costs.** Figure three meals times the number of days you'll be there. Don't forget to include tips, drinks, and so on. Don't skimp, either—you won't be able to enjoy a white-sand getaway if you're starving.

- **Factor in some extra spending.** Souvenirs, fun extras like spa visits or guided tours, unexpected expenses, and so on. If possible, this number should be 10% to 20% of your total budget.

- **Add it all up.** Compare that figure to the amount you have to spend. You're either in good shape or you need to start revising your plan to cut costs.

Keeping Costs Down

- **Consider a honeymoon registry.** Some travel agencies can set up a registry service, allowing wedding guests to help offset your budget in lieu of a physical gift.

- **Go off-season.** You can save heaps by honeymooning to places that aren't in the midst of peak season. The holidays and spring breaks are likely to be busiest, as are long weekends and Valentine's Day.

- **Keep it local.** Fantastic destinations are surely within a few hours' drive of your home. Seek out those hidden gems for a magical experience that doesn't consume your entire budget. (And never underestimate the romance of a night in a fancy nearby hotel.)

- **Speak up!** You don't need to accept the first rate that's quoted. Make it clear you're shopping around and you will be offered better deals.

- **If you're leaving the country, watch the exchange rates.** Bad ones can slice your

budget to ribbons; favorable ones can
stretch your dollars.

- **A room without a view.** Book a corner
room or one facing an interior courtyard.
You'll be spending your time either in bed
or outdoors, anyway.

- **Tell the staff that you're newlyweds.**
Don't be shy about it! Many hotels and
resorts offer discounts or special extras and
upgrades for honeymooners.

- **Eat in.** Not only is it budget friendly to take
a few meals in, preparing a meal together in
your cabin or bungalow can be a romantic
prelude to the best kind of honeymoon fun.

How to Write Thank-You Notes

Dozens of people jumped through hoops to share an important day with you. Some even gave you money and gifts. You have to say thank you—and yes, you have to write more than those two words. Now's the time to express your gratitude.

- **Pick out your thank-you cards as soon as you register for gifts.** Many stationery stores will sell you blank cards that match your invitations. Otherwise, simple, folded ivory paper is traditional (be sure to get envelopes that match). Never use pre-printed messages; if you're old enough to get married, you're old enough to write your own notes. E-mail thank-yous are out of the question.

- **Once you're hitched, don't waste time:** thank-you notes should be sent within three months of the wedding or your return from the honeymoon.

- **Find a comfortable spot with lots of open space.** Kitchen table, bar top, something like that. Have your pile of gifts at hand.

- **Grab the invitation list you made way back when** (page 46). As you open the gifts, jot down the gift next to the person's name.

- **Get writing!** You'll be doing a lot of these, so keep it simple. An example: "Thank you for your generous gift. We're so glad we got to celebrate our wedding with you."

- **Be specific when appropriate.** Unusual or generous gifts, or gifts from a close friend or family member, demand a bit of personalization. "That bronze John Elway statue will look great in our den!"

- **Remember, it's "we" now, not "I."**

- **If you can't remember what you got from one of your guests,** set aside the name for now and follow up later with the store where you were registered. Often, the staff can figure out who bought you what.

- **Sign off with "sincerely" or "best regards."** Family members or close friends can get a "love," but reserve "peace out" for e-mails to your bros.

- **Share the card-writing duties.** Your wife can do the cards for the people closest to her, and you do yours, but always mention the other person, too.

- **With each note you write, check the person's name off that guest list.**

- **When you're done, pour a drink.** Or three. You'll need it.

Six More Questions Everyone's Going to Start Asking You

Did you really think that just because your wedding day has come and gone, you'll stop bearing the brunt of incessant questions? Think again. Now that you've tied the knot, get ready to hear a whole new set of questions over and over and over again.

Remember, the ultimate shut-down response for an awkward question is, "Why do you ask?" Say it politely and watch your nosy interrogator backpedal like crazy.

1. **"So when are you having kids?"**
   Perhaps the most intrusive question you can ask a couple, and it's the one you'll be asked more than any other. If you have no news to offer, simply smile and say, "When we're ready."

2. **"Where did you go for your honeymoon?"**
   The first time you tell the story you'll enjoy reliving the memories. By the

twenty-seventh time, you'll be ready to
run for the hills. Brace yourself.

3. **"So how's the sex life?"**
    Yes, you really will be asked some varia-
    tions of this question. People are fascinat-
    ed with myths about marital sex, probably
    to laugh off shortcomings in their own
    relationship. "Great!" is the only answer
    you ever need to give.

4. **"How much did your wedding cost?"**
    Your wedding was awesome. The price tag
    probably was, too. But it's not anyone's
    business. Have a joke ("I have no idea!
    Guess we'll find out soon!") or a non-
    answer prepared to deflect the attention.

5. **"When will you start looking for a house?"**
    If you already own a home, congratula-
    tions, you get to skip this one. Otherwise,
    people will be eager to push you toward
    your next life milestone. Don't let anyone
    pressure you.

6. **"So when's the divorce party?"**
   People who drop comments like this actually think they're being funny. Or maybe it's a passive-aggressive ploy by someone who doesn't approve of your bride. Either way, don't dignify it.

How to Have Good (Married) Sex

Perhaps the most insidious marriage myth is that your sex life comes to a screeching halt. Sure, you'll run into periodic problems—schedules don't sync up, she feels unsexy after having a child, your newfound beer gut is making you sluggish—but these are not marriage-specific issues. Your married sex life can, and will, be amazing. Just keep these tips in mind.

- **Feel the bond.** You are now a single unit. Immerse yourself in that notion when making love to take your lovemaking to places you never imagined.

- **Your brain is a sex organ.** Physicality is only one part of sex. You know your partner better than anyone; use your head, get into hers, and provide the experience she needs at that moment (slow and close when she needs a connection, a fast afternoon delight when she wants to feel wild, and so on).

- **Rediscover foreplay.** As a married couple, you've already become notches in each other's bedposts, so why not take your time? Spend an hour engaging in nothing but foreplay. Tease, taunt, and tantalize with no thought of whether you ever get to the sex part. You'll feel like teenagers again.

- **Flirt with each other, a lot.** Sexy texts throughout the day (just double-check that number!) can make your partner feel desired, a feeling that occasionally fades after marriage because you're no longer actively pursuing her. So remind her that she still sends shivers up your spine.

- **Be unafraid of schedule changes.** When you settle into a routine, you may find that your work or sleep schedules don't sync up. If you used to get frisky in the evening but no longer, ignite the fire in the morning, before dinner, whenever. The only "right" time is when you're both in the mood.

- **Be unafraid, period.** You get used to each other. You fall into routines. It happens.

Use that close bond to share, experiment, talk frankly about your wants, and try new things. Introduce toys to your playtime. Play dress up. Watch a racy movie together. Be fearless.

- **Get out of the house.** A day trip to a lakeside cottage or a hotel room at a vineyard, anything to take you away from your usual environment. The new setting will help remind you both how much you enjoy getting together under the sheets.

- **Get the kids out of the house.** Perhaps the biggest obstacle to regular, satisfying married sex is children. Don't let this happen. Babysitters exist for a reason!

- **Don't assume you know each other.** You may have had a great premarriage sex life, but you each may still have desires the other doesn't know about. So explore!

- **Don't boast.** Bragging about your sexual exploits is as American as apple pie (there's probably a movie joke in there somewhere). But though telling buddies about your sexual (mis)adventures is par for the course when it comes to flings and girlfriends, things change when you become a married man. Being proud to have an active sex life is natural, but the guys don't need to know what your wife is and is not willing to do in bed. Keep it classy.

How to Say You're Sorry

Apologizing sucks—especially when you have to apologize to your wife. Even for the best of men, it stings. Here's how to beg her pardon and take responsibility for all your wrongdoing.

- **Be sincere.** If it's a big apology—heck, even if it's small—make it formal. Sit her down and talk face-to-face. Don't e-mail or text to say your sorry.

- **Make her feel loved.** Pour her a glass of wine or a cup of tea. Whatever will help her comfortable and secure.

- **Express remorse.** And get right to it. Be brief and to the point. (Hint: start with "I'm sorry.")

- **Listen.** Understand her emotions. If you're apologizing, it's because you hurt her. Show you know how you hurt her by addressing the way she feels, not by simply acknowledging that she's angry.

- **Express your emotions.** It's not enough to understand hers; express your own. Some women respond to emotion in ways many men don't. It will show your sincerity.

- **Don't explain or justify.** The moment of an apology is not the time to explain why you did/said what you did. Save it for later.

- **Don't argue.** Now is also not the time to be drawn into an argument. If she's still ready for a fight, walk away and revisit things later.

- **Man up.** Avoid half-assed apologies like, "I'm sorry you feel that way" or "I'm sorry you got upset." Take responsibility for yourself and don't deflect from your own culpability.

- **Finish with "I love you."** She'll probably need to hear it.

Ten (or So) Small but Essential Courtesies

Here's the dirty little secret that advice-book authors don't want you to know: the small courtesies we take for granted every day are far more important than heart-to-heart talks, counseling sessions, and expensive gestures meant to declare your eternal adoration. Make these habits part of your daily lives to keep the bond strong and the relationship a loving one.

- **Whenever you get yourself a drink, ask if she'd like one, too.**
- **Any time she cooks, wash the dishes.** Any time *you* cook, wash the dishes.
- **Always hold the door for her.**
- **In the bedroom, reciprocate.**
- **Before sitting down at a restaurant, pull out her chair.** Also, she gets the choice of seat, everywhere (airplanes, movies, stadiums, *everywhere*).

- If she's had a bad day, bring home her **favorite ice cream or flowers or treats.**

- **Compliment her. Often.** And do so in front of other people.

- **When socializing with people she's never met, introduce her. Immediately.** Don't assume she'll figure out who's who or that people will know who she is.

- **Don't wait for her to ask you to carry heavy bags/boxes/objects.** Relieve her of these burdens automatically.

- **If she sneezes, get her a tissue before she has a chance to grab one herself.**

- **In the bathroom, use matches to remove unpleasant odors** (they work better than a spray). And replace the toilet paper roll.

- **"Thank you" and "you're welcome."** Always.

Acknowledgments

My thanks to Blair and the staff at Quirk for making me look better at this than I actually am; to Stephen, whose endless support opened this door for me in the first place; to the Refugees (you know who you are), who keep me filled with ideas and energy; and to Robert and Natalie, who are the reason I keep trying.